T0094475

RHAPSODOMANCY

kevin mcpherson eckhoff

Coach House Books, Toronto

Published with the generous assistance of the Canada Council
for the Arts and the Ontario Arts Council. Coach House
Books also acknowledges the support of the Government of
Canada through the Book Publishing Industry Development
Program and the Government of Ontario through the Ontario
Book Publishing Tax Credit.

LIBRARY AND ARCHIVES CANADA

CATALOGUING IN PUBLICATION

McPherson Eckhoff, Kevin, 1981-
Rhapsodomancy / kevin mcpherson eckhoff.

Poems.
ISBN 978-1-55245-231-8

I. Title.

PS8625.P537R53 2010   C811'.6   C2010-900031-5

Table of Contents

'View in these pages – like a mirror bright,
That art divine, now bursting on your sight!
In charms like those of peerless Beauty's smile –
That won the heart it seeks not to beguile!
See in this book the wonderous plan reveal'd
Which heaven from mortals hath till now conceal'd!
Trace in each page the ready writer's mind,
'Tis here his shorthand secrets are divined.'

– James Henry Lewis

INAUGURAL AUGURIES

Sure Sense or Censure?

portrait of a dumbfounder

Rosetta Stone

Pitman's shorthand, Malone's Unifon and English

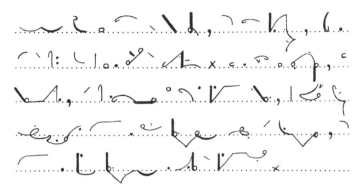

NUฅIⱮ WUTEVƎR IZ MQR TU BⱵ DIZⱵRD, QR MQR DILⱵTFUL, ℏAN ℏU LⱵT UF TRUℏ: FQR IT IZ ℏU SQRS UF WISDUM. WEN ℏU MⱵND IZ HⱯRASD, WIℏ OBSKƎRITⱵ, DISTRAKTED BⱵ DQTS, RENDƎRD TQRPID QR SADEND BⱵ IGNQRANS QR FⱯLSITⱵS, AND TRUℏ IMERJES AZ FRUM Ɐ DⱯRK ABIS, IT 8ⱵNZ FQRℏ INSTANTⱯNEUSLⱵ, LⱵK ℏU SUN DISPƎRIⱮ MISTS AND VⱯPƎRS, QR LⱵK ℏU DⱯN DISPELIⱮ ℏU 8ⱯDS UF DⱯRKNIS.

Nothing whatever is more to be desired, or more delightful, than the light of truth: for it is the source of wisdom. When the mind is harassed, with obscurity, distracted by doubts, rendered torpid or saddened by ignorance or falsities, and truth emerges as from a dark abyss, it shines forth instantaneously, like the sun dispersing mists and vapours, or like the dawn dispelling the shades of darkness.

Shorthanded Unifon

chup chab choob swaddush awleffuh
edz hittoke keckoke kacondoke ktuh
lafush tud ktokonk uttuconguh fod
taconpo deg tockonideah tapat tachater
thez hathconhez muckonnun luckonsh fuconer
swut dairconpuh amdvinga mawdfoon eckond
atrawt dukkond efconsheh hefconhash
paj pokonuj pudt kapk gorog

Writing Lessens

In this brief introduction to Pitman's method of Shorthand, several symbols will be presented in place ⟨⟩ the usual longhand alphabet. Without any previous instruction ⟨⟩ Shorthand, you will ⟨⟩ able to begin reading some of these signs on this page. ⟨⟩ Shorthand writing, some words ⟨⟩ represented using short forms, such as ⟨⟩ one. These abbreviations exist ⟨⟩ single symbols. Other words ⟨⟩ written using a combination ⟨⟩ strokes, just ⟨⟩ ⟨⟩ longhand a word ⟨⟩ constructed ⟨⟩ ⟨⟩ combination ⟨⟩ alphabetic characters. Writing ⟨⟩ ⟨⟩ ⟨⟩ faster ⟨⟩ more efficient ⟨⟩ traditional longhand because ⟨⟩ signs ⟨⟩ much shorter ⟨⟩ simpler ⟨⟩ because ⟨⟩ ⟨⟩, ⟨⟩ sound ⟨⟩ ⟨⟩ word ⟨⟩ represented. ⟨⟩ ⟨⟩ reasons, ⟨⟩ ⟨⟩ ⟨⟩ ideal ⟨⟩ stenographic purposes. ⟨⟩ ⟨⟩ ⟨⟩ learning ⟨⟩ save ⟨⟩ ⟨⟩ time ⟨⟩ money, ⟨⟩, ⟨⟩ ⟨⟩, ⟨⟩ ⟨⟩ record ⟨⟩ human voice ⟨⟩ naturally ⟨⟩ accurately.

Palming the P …

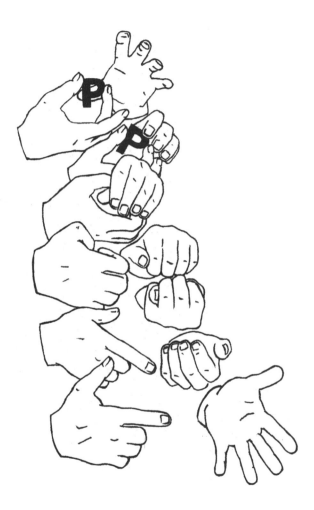

UNSOUND WRITING

'In a smooth train thy mystic figures flow,
And swiftest gales of eastern winds outgo;
Thy pen our words paints with the nicest care
Before the fleeting voice dissolves in air;
Flying as it draws the image of the mind,
Nor one idea wandering leaves behind.
Faithful as echo thy rare art is found,
Preserves the sense as it returns the sound.'

– Anonymous

Ursonate

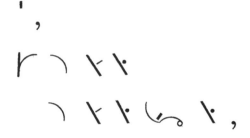

Tema 1

Tema 2

Tema 3

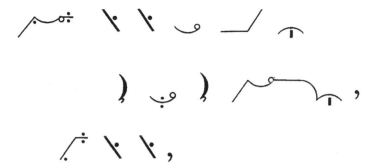

Tema 4

Karawane

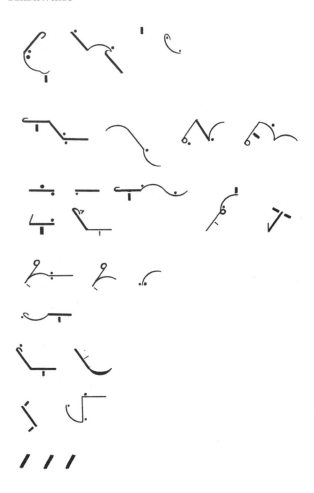

Glossolalia

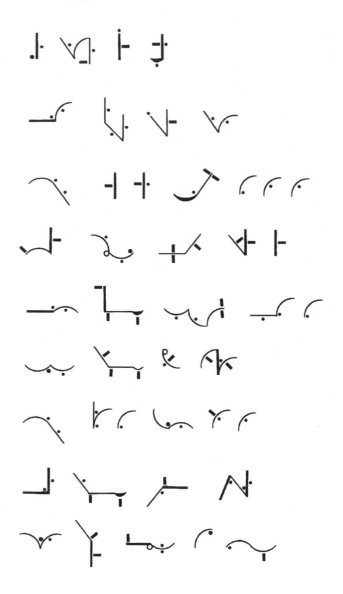

DISAVOWALS:
OPTICAL ALLUSIONS

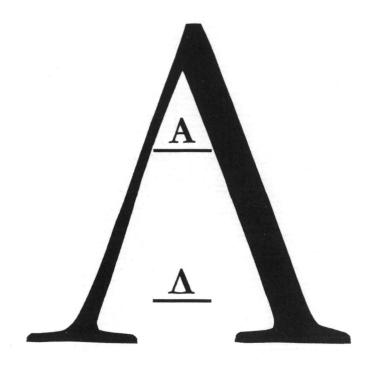

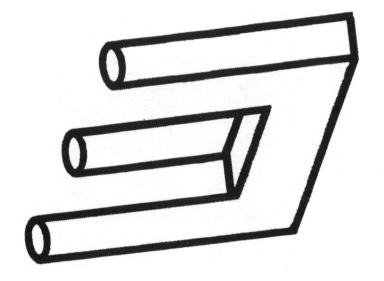

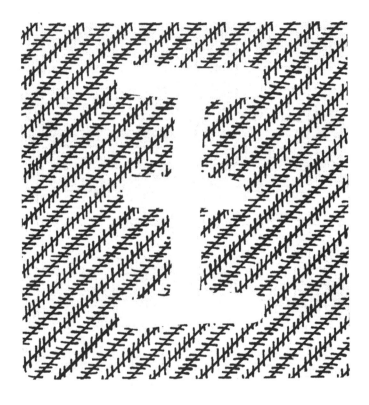

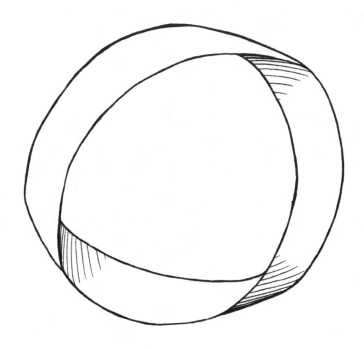

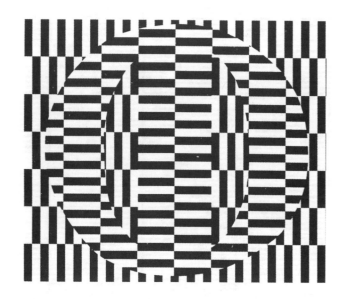

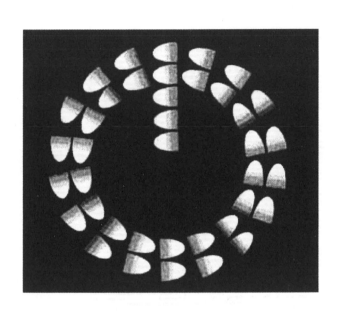

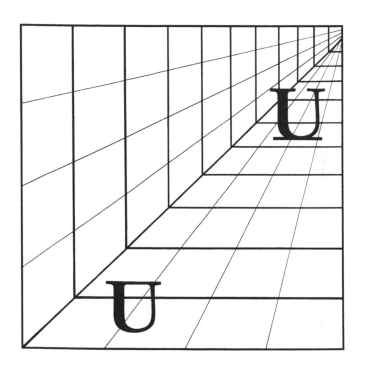

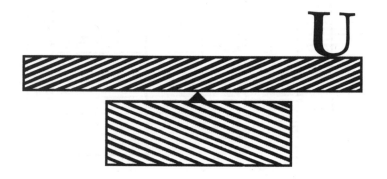

U

Y

●

Close right eye and stare at the dot. Hold paper about twenty centimetres from face and then slowly pull away.

APANTOMANCY

Chiromancy

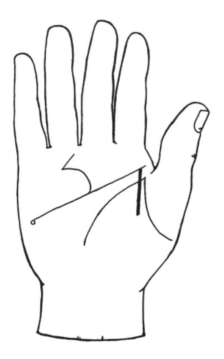

Cubomancy

after Stéphane Mallarmé

a throw of the dice will never abolish chants

Logomancy: trigrammaton

other than this

old word yard,

art or order

are much, and

limit line land.

she shall wish

for fear, far

from free information,

specially subjected speak.

why, how I

want one wonderful

sign soon sent,

coal colour, came

cold call, equal.

take talk tax,

advantage difficult, down

think, thank, thought,

tried toward truth

Logomancy: tetragrammaton

who ought judge large

recent writing? wrong reason.

he itches high, each

built able belief, blew

the a, is, as

principle, particular, probable. opportunity:

doubt idea, die out.

according great cry, grow

long, longer, love left.

rather, our writer should

but commit at it,

her home now here,

whether where white weather

might meet matter, me,

mine, my mind, kind.

with what would you

letter law – low light

right – represent, rate, write?

Logomancy: pentagrammaton

⌣ ‿ ‿ ⌣ ⌣   language thing under hand, owning

‿ ‿ ‿ ‿ ‿   not another note, no know,

ˈ | | ǀ | owe dollar, had different day.

✓ ✓ ✓ ✓ ✓   we wait away, weigh weight,

\ \ ˋ \ ` \   buy, publish, to put by public.

Extispicy

for C. W. Hart

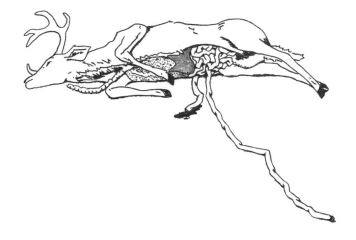

Geomancy I

for Steve McCaffery

the law is of a light who can come at me.
shalt theatre, fah, art too, lfch!
nature, she sure should fatter with thee.
lo, but for thought, thou are recounted.

Geomancy II

for bpNichol

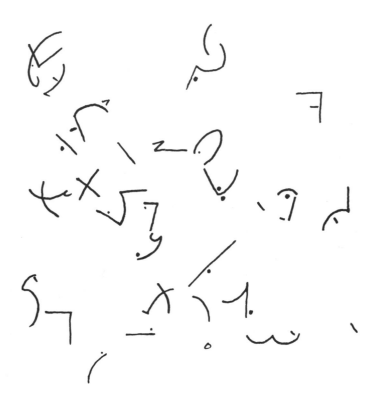

pure hush, thrill. think chains cut, apt opium.
put oik! lash pshaw! new form, our party, pesk.
catch leash to meat, ouch! loot lots, act.
i will arrange reader, err. shitty.
ick, ill is nun, all light.

Lecanomancy

what art is without law or matter
      beyond that sound language, light or neither
         when the word for your nature
            has no home no future
               would a thought see new letters
                as you might know order

Ornithomancy
after Wallace Stevens

solve:

only knowing oral form
limit any other field for this fuller mile
free any other bird for this little faith
order any other army for this unfair minimum
confirm any other method for this immediate animal
never value error for this assumed formality
follow nothing for this needing middle

fully owning enough order
assure any other limit for this failed english
feel any other zeal for this awful fault
share any other reminder for this ended life
fail any other value for this animal material
never form an estimate for this esteemed pharmacy
leave anything for this informed laugh

naturally avoiding myth
never remit

Molybdomancy

apologies to Darren Wershler–Henry

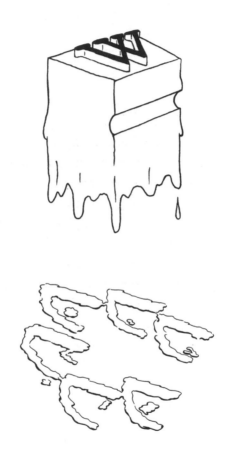

laid lead lied, allowed lewd lode

Phyllorhodomancy

Who is Gertrude Stein?

a rose is a rose is a rose is a ruse

Sideromancy

after Orpheus & his lyre

each air heats itself

Synastry

SAGITTARIUS

world

SCORPIO

truth during direct

LIBRA

success can

VIRGO

free or these arrangements

LEO

distance method

CANCER

mass sign seen sound

GEMINI

    take talk qualities

TAURUS

    especially as

ARIES

    self-control

PISCES

    ask them think

AQUARIUS

    how might eye
    doubt beyond you

CAPRICORN

    who expresses

MUMBLE GIRLS

GORDIAN DÉNOUEMENT

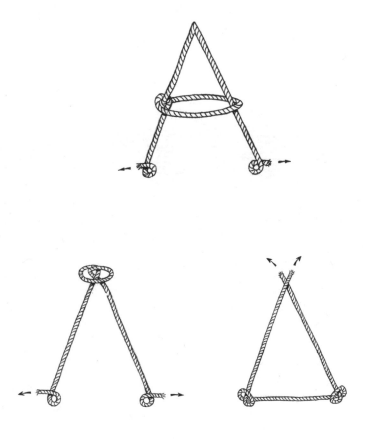

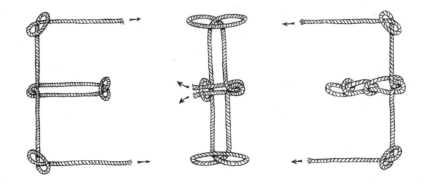

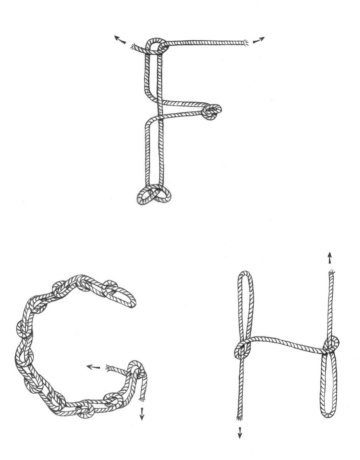

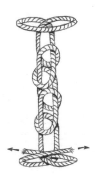

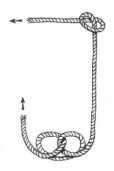

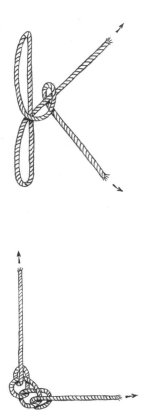

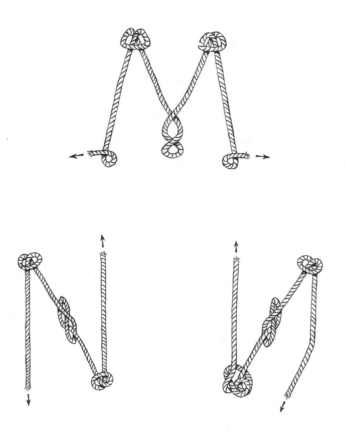

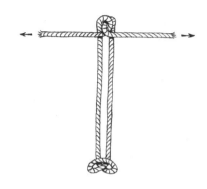

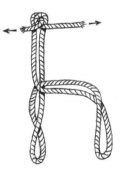

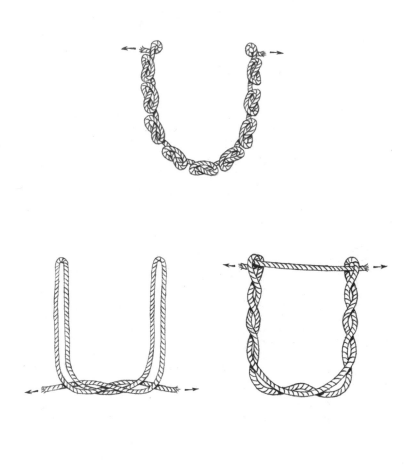

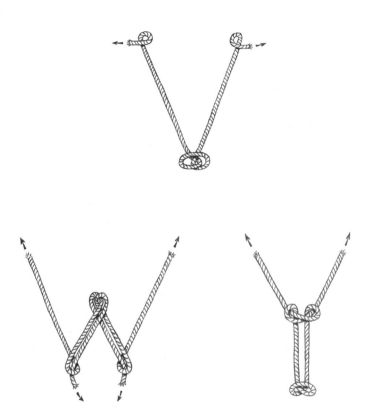

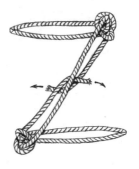

Bibliomancy: notes on the manuscript

> 'Have not poetry and music arisen, as it seems, out of the sounds the enchanters made to help their imagination to enchant, to charm, to bind with a spell themselves and passers-by?'
>
> — William Butler Yeats, 'Magic'

> 'I have no intention of becoming a shorthand author.'
>
> — Sir Isaac Pitman

This project responds to two very obscure endeavours. Have you heard of John Malone's Unifon? Do you remember Sir Isaac Pitman's Shorthand? These two scripts attempted to replace the English alphabet with a complete and accurate visual system of phonetics. Both inventors struggled to reconcile the same dilemma: the English language contains approximately forty phonemes, but its alphabet features only twenty-six graphemes. They viewed this discrepancy as imperfect. Pitman's goals were expediency and purity of vocal expression. He felt his charge was divine: to 'scatter the seeds of truth,' 'rectify error' and 'replace evil with good.' Malone's goal was to create a means of universal communication for the airline industry. When this failed, he marketed Unifon as a reading tool for children. The goals of my project are none of the above. I like to explore.

INAUGURAL AUGURIES

Sure Sense or Censure?

The caption below Sir Isaac Pitman's portrait paraphrases, in Shorthand, an observation from Derrida on Heidegger. It reads: *The voice of being is silent.*

Rosetta Stone
Like Malone, Pitman experimented with Romanesque phonetic alphabets, but decided they were too slow to write. He often used this excerpt from eighteenth-century Swedish mystic Emanuel Swedenborg to present the differences among his frequently improving versions of Shorthand.

Shorthanded Unifon
What if the Unifon alphabet were drawn using Shorthand markings? What if these markings were then transcribed for their phonetic output?

Writing Lessens
Learning Shorthand can be easy, fun and diminishing!

Palming the P ...
Language disappears into the body. Both Malone and Pitman tried to depict the voice, as they believed it to be a vehicle for truth. American Sign Language uses the body as writing, and this piece intertwines the words *palm* and *poem*.

UNSOUND WRITING

For Pitman, the voice lies closer to the mind and to meaning than does writing. However, his phonetic writing system has become unreadable to contemporary eyes and, as such, completely divorced from meaning. Only imagination can read his silent writing now. Similarly, sound poetry often attempts to transcend syntax, words and meaning in order to express unmitigated thought and emotion. The sounds in 'Ursonate,' 'Karawane' and 'Glossolalia' not only resist linguistic logic, they also resonate with that pure sense of the voice that Shorthand claims to record.

'In art alone it still happens that man, consumed by his wishes, produces something similar to the gratification of these wishes, and this playing, thanks to artistic illusion, calls for the effects as if it were something real.'
> – Sigmund Freud, 'Animism, Magic and the Omnipotence of Thoughts'

Optical illusions constitute a form of art that deliberately interrogates our perceptions. Through words, sentences, paragraphs, books, etc., writers express their perceptions of reality. But what reality does an isolated letter represent? Many abjad alphabets, such as Phoenician, Hebrew and Arabic, possess no symbols for vowel sounds – their presence is presupposed. Unifon, conversely, contains sixteen vowel signs, one for each vowel sound, long and short, in the English language. The idea of one perfect symbol for each sound is an illusion because it overlooks the limits of perception. As Gianni A. Sarcone and Marie-Jo Waeber remind us in their introduction to *New Optical Illusions*: 'All inputs to the brain are, to one degree or another, ambiguous [and allow for] multiple interpretations. That's the reason why we have poets.'

APANTOMANCY

'There's nothing religious in any of these matters
In the superstitions or in the prophecies
Or in anything that people call the occult
There is above all a way of observing nature
And of interpreting nature
Which is completely legitimate'
> – Guillaume Apollinaire, 'On Prophecies'

'Apantomancy' refers to divination through whatever objects lie at hand. These poems imagine a relationship between Shorthand and divination, which seeks to make sense of the world by reading for traces of heavenly knowledge within particular objects or actions. The practices of Shorthand and divination seem to me analogous to those of the poet.

Chiromancy: Divination through the palm. When the heart and life lines connect in the centre of the palm, it suggests a hurried character.

Cubomancy: Divination through dice. Stéphane Mallarmé: 'The pure work implies the disappearance of the poet as speaker, who hands over to the words.'

Logomancy: Divination through letters. These visual echoes offer a partial gloss of Shorthand.

Extispicy: Divination through viscera. A pioneer of the tractor, C. W. Hart founded a tractor manufacturing company that was eventually bought out by the John Deere Co. The deer's entrails form the Shorthand symbol for the sound 'awful' or 'offal.'

Geomancy I and II: Divination through dirt thrown to the ground or marks on paper. These symbols, made with closed eyes, have been read as Shorthand inscriptions.

Lecanomancy: Divination through water. All writing ripples and repels.

Ornithomancy: Divination through the flight patterns, wing sounds and songs of birds.

Molybdomancy: Divination through molten metal.

Phyllorhodomancy: Divination through the sound of clapping rose petals.

Sideromancy: Divination through stars. Orpheus could soothe any beast by singing and playing upon his lyre. When the Maenads stoned him, the rocks refused to disrupt such beautiful sounds. The Muses honoured him at his death by throwing his lyre into the heavens.

Synastry: Divination through astral alignment. Shorthand pictograms offer missed fortunes.

MUMBLE GIRLS

'Is there a knowledge, and, above all, a language [...]
that one can call alien at once to writing and violence?'
— Jacques Derrida, 'The Violence of the Letter'

In 2000, Lea Hernandez published the futuristic graphic narrative series *Rumble Girls*, in which she uses a version of Unifon to mark corporate authority. In my interpretation of her text, I transcribe the onomatopoeia from the original comic into Unifon and place it in the mouths, or rather, the suits of the corporate antagonists.

GORDIAN DÉNOUEMENT

'the voice draws their pencil
like a sled across snow; when its runners are frozen
rope snaps and the voice then is pulling no burden'
— P. K. Page, 'The Stenographers'

Three Notes on Knots

Quipu is suspected to be an ancient Incan system of writing composed as knots on connected strands of rope. Most of the recovered Quipu remain undeciphered.

When faced with the Gordian Knot, which was prophesized to reveal the new leader of Asia, Alexander the Great sliced it apart with his sword, declaring, 'I have undone it!'

Treated as entire poem in itself, the Unifon alphabet appears here as a series of looped and tethered ropes that, if pulled, would unravel into unknotted strands.

CREDITS

Both the excerpt from James Henry Lewis's poem and the anonymous verse introducing the 'Unsound Writing' section come from Sir Isaac Pitman's *The History of Shorthand*. The essay on 'Magic' by William Butler Yeats can be found in *The Collected Works of W. B. Yeats: Volume IV*. The line from Isaac Pitman denying his role as an author appears in the book *The Life of Sir Isaac Pitman* by Alfred Baker. Sigmund Freud's quote on animism comes from his *Totem and Taboo*, while Apollinaire's 'On Prophecies' originates in *Calligrammes*. The quote by Stéphane Mallarmé can be read in his collection *The Poems*, translated by Keith Bosley. Jacques Derrida's question appears in *Of Grammatology*, and P. K. Page's poem 'The Stenographers' originally appeared in a collection of her work titled *As Ten as Twenty*.

Acknowledgements

Poems from *Rhapsodomancy* have appeared about town. Much thanks to No Press for two chapbooks, *Selected Rhapsodomancies* and *Gordian Dénouement*. Happy gratitudes to Jake Kennedy, Paola Poletto and Tightrope Books for giving 'Mumble Girls' some pages in *Boredom Fighters*. And thanks to *dandelion* for liking 'Disavowals' enough to print some of them.

This exploration would have been impossible without the following bodies and spirits: Alana Wilcox, Barb Howe, Christian Bök, Craig McLuckie, derek beaulieu, Evan Munday, Heidi Garnett, Jake Kennedy and Mo and Miss Rae, Jason Dewinetz, Jason and Andrea, John Lent, Dr. Jonathan Ball, Jordan Nail, Judith Jurica and Gallery Vertigo, Julie, Kevin Connolly, Luke and Steph (and Nelson and Winston), Mark and Juan, Mary Ellen Holland, Mom and Dad, Monika Gordon, Natalie Zina Walschots, the Outlaws featuring Kris and Anne and Keith, Peter and Andrea, Riley and Jess, Robyn and Owen, the Rossworn Family, ryan fitzpatrick, Susan Rudy, Tim Walters and Tom Wayman.

This book is dedicated to Laurel for letting me rest on her every time.

About the Author

kevin mcpherson eckhoff's poetry has appeared in the anthology *Rogue Stimulus* and in such magazines as *filling Station* and *Open Letter*. He recently bought a house in Armstrong, British Columbia, where he teaches at Okanagan College and falls asleep at drive-in movies with his partner.

Typeset in Adobe Caslon Pro
Printed and bound at the Coach House on bpNichol Lane

Edited by Kevin Connolly
Designed by Alana Wilcox
Author photo by Laurel Eckhoff McPherson

Coach House Books
80 bpNichol Lane
Toronto ON M5S 3J4

416 979 2217
800 367 6360

mail@chbooks.com
www.chbooks.com